Guidance on permit-to-wo

A guide for the petroleum, chemical and allied industries

HSE Books

Contents

Foreword

This guidance replaces the 1997 revision of *Guidance on permit-to-work systems in the petroleum industry* (ISBN 0 7176 1281 3) which took account of industry experience gained since 1991, and takes into account other relevant guidance, in particular *The safe isolation of plant and equipment.*[1]

This revision builds on previous editions by incorporating recent technical advances (eg electronic permit systems) and good practice identified in the onshore and offshore petroleum industry and onshore chemical and allied industries. It highlights key areas for possible future harmonisation of permit-to-work systems.

This document describes good practice in the use of permit-to-work systems, and as such may be useful to operators using permit-to-work systems as part of a demonstration that risks have been reduced to as low a level as reasonably practicable (ALARP). The guidance is applicable to the onshore and offshore petroleum industry, onshore chemical and allied industries and other industries where permit-to-work systems are used.

The document is primarily written around well-established paper-based permit-to-work systems, but where possible it accounts for the newer medium of electronic-based permit-to-work systems.

Introduction

1   The petroleum, chemical and allied industries store and process large quantities of hazardous substances including flammable and toxic materials, so the potential for serious incidents is clear. To prevent such incidents it is vital that there should be effective management of hazards, including the use of safe systems of work.

2   A permit-to-work system is an integral part of a safe system of work and can help to properly manage the wide range of activities which can take place close together in a small space, such as in a storage area or process plant.

3   When incidents do occur, human factors, such as failure to implement procedures properly, are often a cause. These failures may in turn be attributable to root causes such as a lack of training, instruction, communication or understanding of either the purpose or practical application of permit-to-work systems.

4   Permit-to-work systems form an essential part of the task risk assessment process. When a task is identified an appraisal should be carried out to identify the nature of the task and its associated hazards. Next, the risks associated with the task should be identified together with the necessary controls and precautions to mitigate the risks. The extent of the controls required will depend on the level of risk associated with the task and may include the need for a permit-to-work.

5   A permit-to-work is not simply permission to carry out a dangerous job. It is an essential part of a system which determines how that job can be carried out safely, and helps communicate this to those doing the job. It should not be regarded as an easy way to eliminate hazard or reduce risk. **The issue of a permit does not, by itself, make a job safe** - that can only be achieved by those preparing for the work, those supervising the work and those carrying it out. In addition to the permit-to-work system, other precautions may need to be taken - eg process or electrical isolation, or access barriers - and these will need to be identified in task risk assessments before any work is undertaken. The permit-to-work system should ensure that authorised and competent people have thought about foreseeable risks and that such risks are avoided by using suitable precautions. Those carrying out the job should think about and understand what they are doing to carry out their work safely, and take the necessary precautions for which they have been trained and made responsible.

How to use this document

6   This guidance is intended to provide a basic understanding of what is meant by a permit-to-work system. The advice is of a general nature, and is not intended to be exhaustive. It is essential that it is read in conjunction with the specific instructions and guidance produced by individual companies. In addition, the *Task Risk Assessment*[2] and other guidance published by the Step Change in Safety initiative, and guidance published by the Health and Safety Executive (HSE) (see Further reading) should be consulted as appropriate.

7   This guidance is designed to assist in three basic ways:

- to enable assessment of current permit-to-work systems against the principles put forward in this document, and to help to identify improvements to those systems in-line with current good practice;
- to offer guidance on harmonisation of permit-to-work formats and terminology to assist people who regularly travel from site to site, from company to company, from refinery to offshore installation, and may have to work under several systems;
- to allow development of a new permit-to-work system based on current good practice, and to give ongoing guidance through implementation and continued application.

8   This guide includes recommendations based on good practice from the petroleum, chemical and allied industries and learning from the investigation of incidents and accidents involving failures in permit-to-work systems. Some case studies are highlighted in the text. In particular, readers are reminded of the importance of failures in the permit-to-work system in the sequence of events leading up to the Piper Alpha disaster in 1988, as summarised in the subsequent report by the Hon Lord Cullen.[3]

What is a permit-to-work system?

9   A permit-to-work system is a formal recorded process used to control work which is identified as potentially hazardous. It is also a means of communication between site/installation management, plant supervisors and operators and those who carry out the hazardous work. Essential features of permit-to-work systems are:

■   clear identification of who may authorise particular jobs (and any limits to their authority) and who is responsible for specifying the necessary precautions;
■   training and instruction in the issue, use and closure of permits;
■   monitoring and auditing to ensure that the system works as intended;
■   clear identification of the types of work considered hazardous;
■   clear and standardised identification of tasks, risk assessments, permitted task duration and supplemental or simultaneous activity and control measures.

Case study 1
Contractors were engaged to demolish redundant oil storage tanks in a tank farm on an oil blending and storage site. A pump house was still in operation in the vicinity of the redundant tanks and the occupier was aware of the fire risk. A method of work was agreed with the contractors which involved cold cutting those parts of the tanks nearest to the pump house and taking them to a safe place on site for hot cutting into smaller pieces. A permit-to-work was not issued and the agreed procedures were not documented. The contractors did not follow the agreement and began hot cutting the tanks close to the pump house. Flammable vapours from the pump house were ignited and the resulting fire caused considerable damage to the plant. Five firemen were taken to hospital suffering from the effects of the fumes.

A permit-to-work should have been issued for this job and the work monitored by the client to make sure the contractor stuck to the agreed method.

---

10   The terms 'permit-to-work', 'permit' or 'work permit' refer to the paper or electronic certificate or form which is used as part of an overall system of work, and which has been devised by a company to meet its specific needs.

11   A permit-to-work system aims to ensure that proper consideration is given to the risks of a particular job or simultaneous activities at site. Whether it is manually or electronically generated, the permit is a detailed document which authorises certain people to carry out specific work at a specific site at a certain time, and which sets out the main precautions needed to complete the job safely.

12   The objectives and functions of such a system can be summarised as:

■   ensuring the proper authorisation of designated work. This may be work of certain types, or work of any type within certain designated areas other than normal operations;
■   making clear to people carrying out the work the exact identity, nature and extent of the job and the hazards involved, and any limitations on the extent of the work and the time during which the job may be carried out;
■   specifying the precautions to be taken, including safe isolation from potential risks such as hazardous substances, electricity and other energy forms (for details of isolation procedures and when they are appropriate see HSE guidance on *The safe isolation of plant and equipment*);[1]
■   ensuring that the person in direct charge of a unit, plant or installation is aware of all hazardous work being done there;
■   providing not only a system of continuous control, but also a record showing that the nature of the work and the precautions needed have been checked by an appropriate person or people;
■   providing for the suitable display of permits (see paragraph 18);
■   providing a procedure for times when work has to be suspended, ie stopped for a period before it is complete (see paragraph 19);
■   providing for the control of work activities that may interact or affect one another (see paragraph 22);
■   providing a formal handover procedure for use when a permit is issued for a period longer than one shift (see paragraph 23);
■   providing a formal hand-back procedure to ensure that the part of the plant affected by the work is in a safe condition and ready for reinstatement (see paragraph 24);
■   providing a process for change, including the evaluation of change on other planned activity, a determination of when hazards need to be reassessed, and a means for controlled communication of change.

13   A permit-to-work system will be more effective if site management and other personnel have been consulted. Imposing systems without consultation can lead to

procedures that do not reflect the needs of maintenance staff, for example. Procedural violations are then more likely.

Case study 2

In September 1992, a jet of flame erupted from an access opening on the side of a batch still at Hickson and Welch, Ltd, Castleford, West Yorkshire. Five people were killed when the flame destroyed a control room adjacent to the still and damaged the nearby office building. The incident happened while a job was underway to rake out a residue that had built up in the still in the 30 years since it entered service. There were a number of failings identified during the HSE investigation including:

- failure to analyse the sludge and the atmosphere in the vessel prior to starting the job;
- failure to control the temperature of the steam used to soften the sludge, resulting in temperatures in excess of 90 °C being applied;
- use of a metal rake in a flammable atmosphere; and
- failure to properly isolate the vessel prior to the job.

A permit-to-work system was in place on the site and two permits were issued, one for removal of the lid to the access opening and one for blanking the still inlet base. No permit was issued for the actual job to be done. Had a permit been issued for the raking out of the residue then the permit-to-work system may have allowed identification of the hazards associated with the job and allowed controls to be put into place that could have prevented the incident.

Case study 3

A release of 40 000 cubic feet of highly flammable material occurred on an offshore installation when a compressor balance line was not isolated during a maintenance operation. A permit-to-work was issued for the job by a maintenance operator. The permit identified the mechanical and electrical isolations necessary but did not specify the process isolations because the issuer was not aware of the necessary process controls.

Case study 4

In the permit-to-work system in place at the time of the Piper Alpha disaster, there was no cross-referencing when the work carried out under one permit affected the work under another. Reliance was placed on the memory of the designated authority.

Case study 5

A fitter was scalded by an escape of high-pressure steam from an open pipe. Two fitters were carrying out work on the pipes under a permit-to-work. The first fitter thought the job was complete and returned the permit to the process operator who opened the steam valve. The second fitter had not completed his part and was still working on the open pipe. The permit-to-work system did not contain a signing off procedure.

When are permit-to-work systems required?

14 Permit-to-work systems should be considered whenever it is intended to carry out work which may adversely affect the safety of personnel, plant or the environment. However, permit-to-work systems should not be applied to all activities, as experience has shown that their overall effectiveness may be weakened. Permits-to-work are not normally required for controlling general visitors to site or routine maintenance tasks in non-hazardous areas.

15 Permit-to-work systems are normally considered most appropriate to:

- non-production work (eg maintenance, repair, inspection, testing, alteration, construction, dismantling, adaptation, modification, cleaning etc);
- non-routine operations;
- jobs where two or more individuals or groups need to co-ordinate activities to complete the job safely;
- jobs where there is a transfer of work and responsibilities from one group to another.

Case study 6
A major vapour cloud explosion at a chemical complex in Passadena, USA in 1989 killed 23 people and injured 300. The incident occurred during maintenance work on a reactor vessel which was being carried out by a maintenance contractor. During the investigation, it was discovered that there was no effective permit-to-work system in operation that applied to both company employees and contractors. This lack of an effective system led to a communication breakdown and work taking place on unisolated plant.

16 Sites and installations should give particular attention to the permit-to-work system during combined or simultaneous operations to ensure that work undertaken does not compromise safety, for example by a mobile drilling unit or support vessel. Combined operations may require the interface of electronic permit-to-work systems with paper-based systems to enable permits to be transmitted or authorised by remote sites.

17 More specifically, the following are examples of types of job where additional permits or certificates (eg isolation certificates - see Appendix 2) should be considered:

- work of any type where heat is used or generated (eg by welding, flame cutting, grinding etc);
- work which may generate sparks or other sources of ignition;
- work which may involve breaking containment of a flammable, toxic or other dangerous substance and/or pressure system;
- work on high voltage electrical equipment or other work on electrical equipment which may give rise to danger;
- entry and work within tanks and other confined spaces;
- work involving the use of hazardous/dangerous substances, including radioactive materials and explosives;
- well intervention;
- diving, including onshore operations near water;
- pressure testing;
- work affecting evacuation, escape or rescue systems;
- work involving temporary equipment, eg generators, welding equipment etc;
- work at height;
- any operation which requires additional precautions or personal protective equipment (PPE) to be in place;
- any other potentially high-risk operation.

More details on permits and certificates typically used for these jobs are given in Appendix 2.

Case study 7
An explosion occurred in a tank containing aqueous waste contaminated with hydrocarbon solvent. Welding work was being carried out on pipe work supports carrying pipes which led to the top of the tank. The welding ignited fumes in the pipes and the flame spread along the pipes into the tank. Because the work was not being done on pipes containing flammable materials the permit made no reference to the surrounding risks.

Case study 8
Two fitters were sprayed with 98% sulphuric acid while removing an accumulator from an acid pump to repair a seal. Pressure on the discharge side of the pump had not been vented, although their permit-to-work indicated that the line had been cleared. Lack of liaison between the engineering and operating departments over who had done what resulted in the permit being wrongly issued.

Case study 9
A cleaner entered a PVC autoclave to check on the need for cleaning and was overcome by vinyl chloride fumes. The vessel was entered on average twice a week, and although a permit-to-work system had been in place, it had fallen into disuse.

Essentials of permit-to-work systems

Display

18 Copies of a permit-to-work should be clearly displayed:

- at the work site, or in a recognised location near to the work site. (If this is not practicable, eg when a job is carried out in a number of locations, then the permit should be kept on the performing authority); and
- in the central or main control or permit co-ordination room, with additional copies at any local control rooms;
- In addition, a copy of the permit should be kept with the issuing authority, or with the area authority if that person is not located at the worksite or control room.

Case study 10

During the Piper Alpha inquiry it was found that contrary to the written procedure, the performing authority's copy of the permit was frequently not displayed at the job site, and was commonly kept in the performing authority's pocket. Lord Cullen made a specific recommendation on this point:

'Copies of all issued permits should be displayed at a convenient location and in a systematic arrangement such that process operating staff can readily see and check which equipment is under maintenance and not available for operation.'

Suspension

19 Work may sometimes have to be suspended, for example:

- if there is a general alarm;
- for operational reasons, eg when the permit is for hot work and process fluid or gas sampling must be carried out at the same time, with the possibility of a release of a dangerous substance;
- while waiting for spares;
- there is a change to the nature or scope of the work;
- where there is conflict with another scope of work. It is important to remember that a suspended permit remains live until it is cancelled. This means that there may still be active isolations under a suspended permit.

Case study 11

On Piper Alpha suspended permits were kept in the safety office, NOT in the control room, as it was claimed there was not enough room. A lead production operator could be aware of a permit-to-work if it was one of the permits which came to him for suspension in the 45 minutes before he officially came on shift. However, it would be completely unknown to him if it had been suspended days before, or earlier on the same day before he arrived in the control room for the handover. The correlation of suspended and active permits was made more difficult by the fact that in the safety office, suspended permits were filed according to trade involved rather than location. This made it difficult for any supervisor to readily check which equipment was isolated for maintenance.

It was also found that there were often large numbers of suspended permits, some of which had been suspended for months eg in February 1998, five months before the disaster, 124 permits-to-work were found to be outstanding. This added to the difficulty of checking which equipment was undergoing maintenance.

20 Suspended permits should be kept on the permit recording system. In addition, the condition in which the plant has been left and the consequences for other activities should be specified. The work should not be restarted until the issuing authority (see paragraph 29) has verified that it is safe to do so, and has revalidated the permit or issued a new permit. If work is left under a suspended permit, integrity of safety systems or the security of any isolation that has been made is important, and the plant should not be assumed to be safe for normal or other use.

21 In other cases the permit may be cancelled, so that as far as the permit-to-work system is concerned, the suspended job is treated as if it were new work when it is restarted. This may be the best option if the suspension of work is indefinite and the plant can be brought to a safe condition.

Permit interaction

22 It is important to make sure that one activity under a permit-to-work does not create danger for another, even if the other work does not require a permit-to-work. Those involved with the issue of permits-to-work should be aware of potential interaction, and should ensure that when a

permit is prepared, the work to be carried out takes account of other activity currently planned or underway. It may be that the interacting activities are covered by separate responsible authorities (see paragraph 29), in which case close liaison will be necessary, for example through cross-referencing on the permit, the task risk assessment or in the work pack. Again, interacting activities may make special demands upon isolation procedures if an isolation is common to more than one job, and isolations should be clearly detailed on the permit or a supporting cross-referenced isolation certificate.

Handover

23   If work is carried over to another shift, eg the job takes longer then expected, then a shift handover procedure should be in place. This handover procedure should ensure that the incoming shift is aware of any outstanding permit-controlled jobs, the status of those jobs, and the status of the plant. Work-in-progress should be left in a condition that can be reliably communicated to, and understood by, the oncoming shift. A permit log, permit file or display boards are ways of recording ongoing permits. It is essential that there is good communication between incoming and outgoing issuing and performing authorities and it is recommended that the incoming issuing authority signs to allow the continuation of a permit.

Case study 12
In his report on the Piper Alpha public inquiry, Lord Cullen found that the handovers between phase 1 operators and maintenance lead hands on the night of the disaster had failed to include communication of the fact that PSV 504 had been removed for overhaul and had not been replaced. This missing PSV was the source of the leak which subsequently ignited.

Hand-back

24   The hand-back procedure should include obtaining answers to the following questions:

- Has the work been completed? This should be confirmed by the performing authority, ie the person to whom the permit was issued.
- Has the plant or equipment been returned to a safe condition, in particular by removing isolations? Has this been verified by the person responsible for signing off

the permit (ie issuing or area authority)?
- Has the person in control of operational activities acknowledged on the permit that the plant or equipment has been returned to the control of the production staff?

Permit authorisation and supervision

25   A permit-to-work system will be fully effective only if the permits are co-ordinated and controlled by an issuing or other responsible authority (see paragraph 29), and there is adequate supervision and monitoring of the system to make sure that the specified procedures are being followed. This should include site visits by the issuing authority to check whether the conditions of the permit are being complied with (as a minimum, at start and completion of the task, with interim checks depending on hazard, complexity and duration of task). Managers or supervisors should not rely solely on scrutinising forms to see whether they have been completed properly, but should carry out additional checks of issuer's forms on a sample basis. Careful consideration should be given to the number of signatures required for a permit. Signatures or 'initials' should only be required where they add value to the safety of the work undertaken, and those signing permits or supporting documentation should have specific training and authorisation from the company.

26   Where the potential for harm is considered to be particularly high, the permit should be seen by a second person (the permit authoriser) before issue, ie the authorisation procedure should be more rigorous. In any case, a person should not issue a permit to themself.

27   Effective supervision of the permit-to-work system can be diluted in the case of a large number of permits under the control of one person. Site management should have arrangements to identify very active periods (eg during plant shutdowns) and assess what steps are necessary to maintain the required supervision, eg either by limiting the number of active permits or by providing additional resource for supervision and co-ordination of permits.

28   The duty holder should ensure the permit-to-work system is properly resourced. Permit issuers need sufficient time to check site conditions (as a minimum, at start and completion of tasks, plus intermediate checks as appropriate), to ensure effective implementation of the system. In particular, high hazard or complex tasks will require a greater degree of monitoring. This will restrict the number of permits a single issuer can manage at any one time.

Case study 13

For a permit-to-work system to function properly it must be managed so that personnel within the system are competent and that responsibility is taken for its management. This case study shows how management failings can lead to serious incidents even where a permit has been issued. Clearly understood responsibilities and adequate training (described later in this guidance) are essential.

Two men employed by a contractor died as a result of an explosion and fire in a horizontal brace in a semi-submersible oil exploration rig while it was undergoing repair at dock in Dundee. The rig operator's permit-to-work system was being used at the time of the incident. The explosion was caused by leaks from a propane hose which the contractors were using for welding and cutting. A fatal accident inquiry was held, at which the sheriff identified a number of failings which could have been put right by reasonable precautions and could have prevented the accident.[4] The failures relating to the operation of the permit-to-work system were found to be;

- Inadequate training;
  - and poor instruction for the tradesmen and labourers working for the contractor in the braces on their roles under the rig operator's permit-to-work system;
  - for the contractor's management and workforce and those responsible for the operation of the permit-to-work system employed by the rig operator, who did not properly understand the system and had not made appropriate provision for its effective operation;
  - for the deputy offshore installation manager (OIM) in the operation of the permit-to-work system;
  - for the general foremen employed by the contractor, who had not been properly instructed in their functions within the permit-to-work system.
- Incompetent management:
  - the operator had not properly considered the competence of the OIM, given his complete lack of understanding of the critical importance of a permit-to-work system, and had not provided him with any support in overseeing the repair work being carried out;
  - the OIM had failed to operate the permit-to-work system properly, work sites had not been inspected, he was not properly aware of the nature of the work being carried out, he had not determined what precautions were necessary, that they were in place and that workers were adequately trained to use them.
- Poor working practices:
  - certificates and permits issued under the permit-to-work system had not been adequately completed and the necessary precautions had not been implemented;
  - the certificates and permits issued under the system were not displayed at the work sites.
- Inadequate communication:
  - neither the rig operator nor the contractor had, at the appropriate management level, established a system for adequate communication between the two companies on safety issues arising in the course of the work, and had not determined who would be responsible for matters such as supervision of the permit-to-work system and the implementation of precautions identified in the risk assessments.

Harmonising roles within permit-to-work systems

29 There are a number of roles which are commonly found in the day-to-day running of permit-to-work systems. There can be considerable variation in the titles given to those people carrying out these roles. Table 1 compares titles used in different permit-to-work systems among companies and business units and suggests a common title for each role. The suggested titles may encourage companies developing new permit-to-work systems to work towards common roles and titles, to promote understanding and consistency and encourage harmonisation, particularly in the offshore sector.

30 In some permit-to-work systems, a number of the roles listed in Table 1 may in fact be fulfilled by the same person, eg on a small site with few permits the same person may act as area authority, issuing authority and permit authoriser at the same time. For this reason, responsibilities given in the next chapter are detailed as they apply to recognisable positions within all industries, with roles highlighted where appropriate.

Role	Suggested title	Alternate titles found in permit-to-work systems
Person requiring the job to be done	Originator	Permit originator, requestor
Person working under the terms of the permit	Permit user	Competent person
Person authorising the permit for issue, eg if an extra level of authorisation is required (see paragraph 26)	Permit authoriser	OIM, approver
Person issuing the permit	Issuing authority	Responsible person, permit co-ordinator, asset shift supervisor, permit issuer
Person accepting the permit on behalf of the permit user(s)	Performing authority	Acceptor, nominated person, work leader, person in charge of the work
Person in control of the location where work is to be carried out	Area authority	Nominated area operator, area authority, responsible person, system operator
Person carrying out checks as detailed on the permit	Site checker	Gas tester, authorised gas tester
Person responsible for making isolations	Isolating authority	Authorised person (electrical, mechanical, process), responsible person (eg responsible electrical person, or electrical responsible person)

Table 1 Comparison of titles for roles within permit-to-work systems

Responsibilities

31 The Management of Health and Safety at Work Regulations 1999[5] outline duties under the Health and Safety at Work etc Act 1974,[6] which relate to the control of work activity and risk assessment. These regulations apply to all workplaces in the UK, including offshore installations. Other legislation makes specific reference to activities that may be controlled by a permit-to-work. Details of relevant legislation are given in Appendix 1.

32 The employer, site occupier or installation duty holder (ie the installation owner or operator) has overall responsibility for ensuring proper permit-to-work systems are developed and followed. But everyone who carries out work of any kind on a site or installation — contractors, subcontractors, in fact all workers — has responsibilities and duties under a permit-to-work system. It is important that each person is adequately trained and knows exactly what those responsibilities and duties are if they are to be carried out properly. (Note: for offshore installations, specific responsibilities are given to the offshore installation manager (OIM). For onshore sites, these responsibilities belong to the duty holder but will often be delegated to the site or plant manager.)

Employers or duty holders

33 The site occupier for onshore installations and the duty holder for an offshore installation should, as appropriate, ensure that:

- a senior manager is assigned responsibility to ensure an appropriate permit-to-work system is introduced;
- appropriate procedures are established and maintained for all work done under the permit-to-work system;
- arrangements are made for the workforce to be made aware of the permits and systems, and trained in their operation;
- the permit-to-work system is monitored to ensure that it is effective and correctly applied;
- the permit-to-work system is audited and reviewed;
- copies of permits, or records of their issue, are kept for a specified period to enable auditing or incident investigation (see paragraph 54);
- sufficient resources are provided to enable the permit-to-work system to be properly implemented.

Site or installation managers (acting as originator, permit authoriser or area authority)

34 As part of their duties, assigned by the site occupier for onshore installations and by the duty holder for offshore installations, the site or offshore installation manager (OIM) should ensure that the above arrangements (paragraph 33) are in place. In addition, the site manager/OIM will take on the following roles or ensure there are arrangements in place which clearly delegate them:

- all work requiring a permit-to-work is identified;
- the permit contains a clear description of the work to be done, its location, start time and duration;
- permits for work activities that may interact or affect other site activity are adequately controlled;
- all other work that would create a hazard if undertaken at the same time is suspended and made safe;
- limitations on the timing and scope of the work are defined as well as actions to be taken in the event of site emergencies;
- all personnel engaged in the preparation of permits, and responsible for the supervision and performance of the work, are identified and competent;
- sufficient information is given to oncoming shifts about work for which there is a permit and which has not been completed;
- all personnel (including contractors) working within the permit system have sufficient knowledge and competence to carry out their duties.

35   It is essential that a competent person (referred to as the 'area authority' in this guidance) is appointed to co-ordinate and control the issue and return of permits. That person should have an overview of all operations under way and planned on site to avoid hazards caused by simultaneous activities. The site or installation manager is normally responsible for ensuring this co-ordination and control, either by controlling the issue and return of permits themselves (a preferable arrangement on smaller offshore platforms or where there are only a small number of permits daily), or by appointing an appropriate responsible person (or people) with sufficient authority to carry out this function on their behalf.

Contractors' and subcontractors' management (acting as performing authority or permit user)

36   The management of contracting companies should:

- ensure that they understand the principles of permit-to-work systems as they are applied in the industry;
- ensure that they understand the permit-to-work systems and other arrangements that apply to the particular locations at which they or their employees are to work;
- ensure that all performing authorities and permit users are properly trained, and understand the permit-to-work systems and any other specific arrangements made for a job, area or location in which they are to work;
- ensure that up-to-date records of trained performing authorities are kept.

Responsible authority (acting as permit authoriser, issuing authority or area authority)

37   The responsible person may also be (among other things) the issuing authority responsible for issuing the permit to the performing authority. For some sites, they may not be the area authority, and should therefore liaise closely with other supervisors or people working in the area. The area authority should know what is being done, especially at critical points such as breaking containment, handover or suspension. The responsible person should ensure that:

- all hazards associated with the proposed job have been identified and suitably assessed;
- all steps necessary to ensure the safety of the site or installation have been identified;
- the work site has been examined, and all precautions specified to be taken before work commences (including isolations) have in fact been taken and will remain effective while the permit remains in force;
- the performing authority is aware of the precautions taken, any additional ones which are to be taken, particular equipment to be used or worn, and any other procedures which are to be followed;
- work activities that may interact or affect one another are clearly identified and either conflict avoided or precautions included on the permit (eg use of welding shields);
- people are aware of the permit's duration, and action to be taken if the work is suspended;
- copies of all issued permits are displayed at an

appropriate location and in a consistent arrangement so that site personnel can readily see and check which equipment is under maintenance and not available for operation;
- the work site is examined at any time when work is suspended and before it is restarted, and finally when the work is completed to ensure that it is in a safe condition;
- the shift handover procedure is properly followed;
- any precautions and isolations are withdrawn at the end of the job unless they are cross-referenced to other permit activity;
- the area authority has acknowledged the return of plant or equipment to their full control.

38   It is essential that people authorised to issue permits-to-work have sufficient knowledge about the hazards associated with the relevant plant, to allow them to identify those hazards and control measures (eg isolations) correctly. If authorised people are relocated to former workstations, then refresher training should be given and recorded before they are reauthorised.

Supervisory personnel (acting as performing authority or permit user)

39   Supervisory staff, whether employed by the employer, duty holder or contractors, should ensure that:

- they and the people working with them understand the operation of (and the consequences of non-compliance with) the permit-to-work systems applicable to the areas in which they are responsible for work;
- any necessary information, instruction or training is given to users to ensure that they understand the permit-to-work systems and the specific precautions required for their work;
- that the performing authority and permit users fully understand their responsibilities under the permit-to-work system;
- the conditions and precautions specified in the permits are fully understood, implemented and effectively monitored;
- the issuing authority is informed when a job has been completed, suspended, if conditions alter or if the task needs to be altered.

Individuals (acting as permit user, site checker or isolating authority)

40   All individuals working at the site or installation should ensure that:

■   they are able to demonstrate a good understanding of the permit-to-work systems that are operated in any location at which they may have to work;

■   they do not start work on any job requiring a permit until one has been authorised and issued, its content understood and necessary precautions taken;

■   the conditions and precautions specified in the permits issued to them, or for work in which they will be involved, are fully implemented and will continue to be effective throughout the duration of work;

■   all the precautions and safety measures that the permits and instructions state they should take are strictly followed;

■   if in any doubt, or if any circumstances or conditions change, they stop work, make the work area safe and get advice immediately.

Training and competence

41   There are many organisational approaches to permit-to-work systems. Permit-to-work systems do not have to be a complex process, but require continual use and practise to reinforce workforce risk awareness and enhance safety performance.

42   Effective training is essential to achieve quality and consistency in the use of the permit-to-work system. There should be successive levels of training for those involved. Training provides the foundation for effective implementation of a permit-to-work system and supports user competence. Training is the first step for permit-to-work users — the continued participation of all relevant people is necessary to improve understanding and system ownership.

43   Operators should take opportunities to share training where appropriate, to encourage good practice and the harmonisation of permit-to-work systems:

- **Why:**
- to ensure that all relevant people are able to become competent and sufficiently involved in the permit-to-work system;
- to ensure understanding of the hazards associated with the working environment and the necessary controls;
- to drive awareness and increase personal levels of risk perception which influence behaviour;
- communicate work site hazards and risks through participation;
- to allow cross-industry sharing – especially of solutions.

- **Who:**
- all workers (at every level of each organisation involved) who actively take part in and contribute towards the permit-to-work system;
- new and transient personnel who may be required to participate in permit activities during their time at site.

- **What:**
- the principles of a permit-to-work system;
- when permits are required;
- an understanding of the types of permits, supporting certificates (see Appendix 2) and other documentation (eg risk assessments and method statements);
- responsibilities and competence requirements for signatories or authorised people within the permit-to-work system. An assessment of competency should cover practical and thinking skills as well as knowledge. Training should focus on use of the permit-to-work system, but must also ensure that the individual understands the working environment, the hazards

associated with it, and more importantly, the controls required to appropriately manage the risks presented by those hazards. These elements of competency need to be demonstrated prior to permit-to-work training for issuers;
- responsibilities of permit users;
- lessons from incidents associated with permits-to-work and findings from audit and review.

- **Where:**
- a quiet area, on site or at a suitable alternative location, for a detailed explanation of the permit-to-work process and the completion of documentation;
- in a classroom, an office, in a variety of environments that will enable the training to be practical in nature and to focus on permit-to-work requirements, types of documentation, hazard identification and necessary site or equipment precautions.

- **When:**
- as part of an induction and prior to undertaking any work authorised under a permit-to-work, to ensure an understanding of the system and enable participation;
- prior to becoming an authorised person for permit-to-work signatures;
- refresher training is required after revalidation of individual competence and after further assessment of competence based on individual needs as required by established company performance standards, eg after a change in the system or following a system audit.

- **How:**
A combination of common training approaches should be employed, including:
- classroom presentations;
- videos;
- mentoring or coaching (eg on-the-job training);
- distance learning;
- practical exercises;
- computer-based training or electronic learning;
- coaching.

44   Once training has been given, competence should be tested to ensure that satisfactory standards have been achieved by the trainees. In addition, competence should be re-tested at appropriate intervals.

45   It is common practice for authorised issuers who are undergoing training to have their permit-to-work countersigned by experienced issuers for a period of time after training, and for a trainee issuer to be asked

to demonstrate an appropriate level of competence to a line manager.

46   Records of training and competence assessments should be kept, as they will be of benefit for recording whether individuals are competent to perform particular roles within permit-to-work systems.

What does a permit-to-work look like?

47 General advice on the design of a permit is given below. Workforce involvement is key to permit design – active input from all categories of personnel who use these documents is necessary to ensure that they are usable and reflect the permit-to-work system in operation. It is emphasised that the purpose of these forms is to support clear and accurate communication between several parties. *Reducing error and influencing behaviour* HSG48[7] provides some general advice on the presentation and layout of procedures and this advice applies equally well to permits. Factors to consider include:

- keep sentences short and simple;
- clearly state **who** does **what** and **when**;
- use colour-coding (eg to illustrate individual roles);
- use the present tense and the active voice;
- do not use text fonts smaller than 8 point;
- place items on the permit in the order they are performed;
- make cross-referencing easy – keep related information together;
- make use of open space in the text – avoid 'clutter';
- use UPPER CASE sparingly for emphasis;
- leave enough room for descriptions (eg to list area involved, hazards and precautions), specifying the level of detail required;
- provide actual quantitative values and limits (eg don't just say 'must not exceed a critical level').

48 The permit-to-work form must help communication between everyone involved. It should be designed by the company issuing the permit, taking into account individual site conditions and requirements. Separate permit forms may be required for different tasks, such as hot work and entry into confined spaces, so that sufficient emphasis can be given to the particular hazards present and the precautions required.

49 The essential elements of a permit-to-work form are shown in Figure 1. If the permit you use does not cover these areas it is unlikely to be fully achieving its purpose. Signatures on permit-to-work forms should be dated and timed.

50 Whatever media are employed at a particular site or installation — paper-based or electronic — it essential that the particular use and types of permit are clear to everyone involved or affected by potentially hazardous work. Wherever possible, permits and hazardous activity certificates should be comprised of *primary* colours - blue, red, or yellow - to promote consistency across the industry. Table 2 gives suggested colours for different types of permit - these colours should be considered when setting up a new permit-to-work. (Note: permits should be white except where specified.) It is suggested that harmonisation of permit colours will be particularly helpful when dealing with a travelling workforce who may regularly work at sites operated by different companies, eg maintenance workers in the offshore sector.

Type of permit or certificate	Suggested colour
Hot work	Red-edged or red
Cold work	Blue-edged or blue
Confined space entry certificate	Green-edged or green
Equipment disjointing certificate/breaking containment permit	Black-edged
Isolation certificate	White
High voltage electrical isolation certificate	Yellow-edged or yellow
Sanction to test certificate	White
Excavation certificate	White
Diving certificate	White (or relevant colour from list above if diver carrying out that type of work)

Table 2 Suggested colours for different types of permits and certificates

1 Permit title	2 Permit reference number Reference to other relevant permits or isolation certificates
3 Job location	
4 Plant identification	
5 Description of work to be done and its limitations	
6 Hazard identification – including residual hazards and hazards associated with the work	
7 Precautions necessary and actions in the event of an emergency – people who carried out precautions, eg isolating authority, should sign that precautions have been taken	
8 Protective equipment (including PPE)	
9 Issue – signature (issuing authority) confirming that isolations have been made and precautions taken, except where these can only be taken during the work. Date and time duration of permit. In the case of high hazard work (paragraph 26) a further signature from the permit authoriser will be needed	
10 Acceptance – signature confirming understanding of work to be done, hazards involved and precautions required. Also confirming permit information has been explained to all permit users	
11 Extension/shift handover procedures – signatures confirming checks made that plant remains safe to be worked upon, and new performing authorities and permit users made fully aware of hazards/precautions. New expiry time given	
12 Hand-back – signed by performing authority certifying work completed. Signed by issuing authority certifying work completed and plant ready for testing and recommissioning	
13 Cancellation – certifying work tested and plant satisfactorily recommissioned	

Figure 1 Essential elements of a permit-to-work form

Electronic permits

51   Permits can be produced electronically and a number of companies are using this type of system. There may be advantages in reducing the amount of paperwork associated with the permit process. However, before introducing an electronic permit system operators must be sure that:

■   a suitable system (eg password-protected electronic signatures) is in place to prevent unauthorised issue or acceptance;
■   permits cannot be issued remotely without a site visit;
■   systems are in place to prevent permits already issued from being altered without the alterations being communicated to all concerned;
■   the facility exists for paper permits to be produced for display at the job site;
■   training is provided to ensure that operators assess the specific job and do not rely on 'cutting and pasting' existing sections from other permits;
■   suitable back-up systems are available in the event of a software failure or power outage.

Work planning and risk assessment

52   Work requiring a permit-to-work is often a non-routine activity. Maintenance tasks and engineering works may require a breach in pressure lines, plant or equipment and can create a hazardous environment.

53   Maintenance instructions or the engineering work pack should refer to relevant procedures, and include necessary drawings and lists of materials required. The management system should ensure that work orders or instructions include an assessment of any risks involved in the task. This could include a preliminary risk assessment, supplemented by a further site risk assessment later when all other tasks planned for the area can be considered.

54   When a permit-to-work activity is identified, the first part of the process should be to determine exactly what the task will involve, including:

■   the need for any special safety studies or assessments (eg task risk assessment, COSHH, manual handling);
■   whether it is obvious that the task cannot be carried out safely, and should be immediately discarded or delayed until other operations due to take place at the same time have been completed. If the likely hazards cannot be reconciled at this stage through task or other risk assessment, then the task should be rejected or redefined;
■   the personal competency requirements needed to undertake the work (or the isolations) or safety support (eg visual support for over-side work, additional personnel for confined space entry).

55   Any work involved in the permit-to-work system, including site surveys and other task or risk assessments necessary, should be part of the integrated planning process for the site. Wherever possible, access should be provided to common industry hazard database information, safety alerts, and industry task risk assessment guidance. If, however, the risk assessment identifies hazards that cannot be addressed, or if the proposed task will pose unacceptable risks for people at the site, then the work should not be permitted. A safer method will need to be identified.

56   A flow diagram illustrating this process is given in Figure 2.

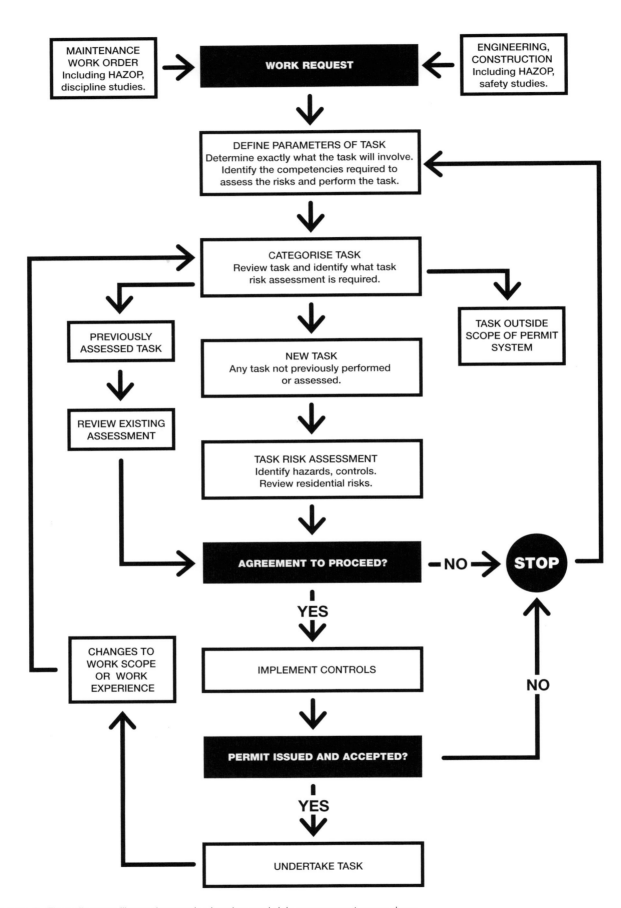

Figure 2 Flow diagram illustrating work planning and risk assessment procedures

Monitoring, audit and review of permit-to-work systems

57   The ultimate success of a permit-to-work system depends on the awareness of the people carrying out the activity. If they do not have a sound understanding of permit or isolation requirements, what it means to them and what their responsibilities are, the system will have a limited effect on preventing accidents.

58   Permits-to-work, certificates and risk assessments should be retained at site by the issuing authority for at least 30 days after completion, and then archived for a specified period to enable an effective monitoring and audit process.

59   In addition to checks carried out by issuers, permit-to-work monitoring checks should be undertaken by site management and supervisors to validate compliance with detailed work instructions and control measures. Information gained from permit monitoring should be used to reinforce safe working practices on site. Monitoring records should be archived on site, and reviewed during periodic permit-to-work audits. A checklist for day-to-day permit monitoring is given in Appendix 4.

60   Permit-to-work systems should be reviewed regularly to assess their effectiveness. This review should include both leading and lagging indicators as well as specific incidents that could relate to inadequate control of work activity. A checklist for the assessment of permit-to-work systems is given in Appendix 3.

61   The permit-to-work system should be audited regularly, by competent people, preferably external to the site or installation and who are familiar with local management system arrangements. The audit process should examine monitoring records. Non-conformance with the permit-to-work system should be recorded, and subsequent remedial measures tracked to ensure all issues are effectively closed out. The checklist in Appendix 3 can be used to audit (or measure) the permit system against relevant good practice.

62   Management should be notified immediately if any non-conformance is identified during routine monitoring or auditing, which cannot be immediately resolved.

63   System reviews, undertaken at least every three years with site and corporate management, should consider audit reports and recent industry information (eg learning from incidents, industry workgroups, safety alerts).

Appendix 1 Relevant legal requirements

Legal requirements relevant to permits-to-work are set out in the following legislation:

Health and Safety at Work etc Act 1974[6]

Section 2   General duties of employers to
               their employees
Section 3   General duties of employers and self-
               employed to people other than their
               employees
Section 7   General duties of employees at work

The Health and Safety at Work etc Act 1974 (HSW Act) applies to work activities carried out at onshore locations and, by virtue of the Health and Safety at Work etc Act 1974 (Application outside Great Britain) Order 1995,[8] to certain activities in territorial waters and the UK sector of the continental shelf.

Confined Spaces Regulations 1997[9]

Regulation 4   Work in confined spaces
Regulation 5   Emergency arrangements

Control of Major Accident Hazards Regulations (COMAH) 1999[10]

Regulation 4   General duty
Regulation 5   Major accident prevention policy
Regulation 7   Safety report

Control of Substances Hazardous to Health Regulations (COSHH) 2002[11]

Regulation 6   Assessment of health risks
Regulation 7   Prevention or control of exposure to
                 substances hazardous to health
Regulation 8   Use of control measures
Regulation 9   Maintenance, examination and test of
                 control measures
Regulation 12   Information, instruction, and training, and
                 training for people who may be exposed to
                 substances hazardous to health

Dangerous Substances and Explosive Atmospheres Regulations 2002[12]

Regulation 5   Risk assessment
Regulation 6   Elimination or reduction of risks from
                 dangerous substances
Regulation 7   Places where explosive atmospheres
                 may occur
Regulation 8   Arrangements to deal with accidents,
                 incidents and emergencies
Regulation 9   Information, instruction and training
Regulation 10   Identification of hazardous contents of
                 containers and pipes
Regulation 11   Duty of co-ordination

Electricity at Work Regulations 1989[13]

Regulation 4(3) General requirement for safe working systems,
                work activities and protective equipment
Regulation 13   Precautions for work on equipment made
                dead. Advice on written procedures is given
                in *Memorandum of guidance on the
                Electricity at Work Regulations 1989.
                Guidance on Regulations* HSR25.[14]

Ionising Radiations Regulations 1999[15]

Lifting Operations and Lifting Equipment Regulations 1998[16]

Regulation 8   Organisation of lifting operations

Management of Health and Safety at Work Regulations 1999[5]

Regulation 3   Risk assessment to determine preventive and
                 protective measures
Regulation 4   Arrangements for effective planning,
                 organisation control, monitoring and review
                 of preventive and protective measures
Regulation 8   Information for employees
Regulation 9   Co-operation and co-ordination
Regulation 10   People working in host employer's undertaking
Regulation 11   Capabilities and training

Offshore Installations (Prevention of Fire and Explosion, and Emergency Response) Regulations 1995[17]

Offshore Installations (Safety Case) Regulations 1992[18]

Regulation 8   Management of health and safety and control of major accident hazards

Offshore Installations and Pipeline Works (Management and Administration) Regulations 1995[19]

Regulation 8   Co-operation
Regulation 10 Permits-to-work
Regulation 11 Instructions

Offshore Installations and Wells (Design and Construction) Regulations 1996[20]

Regulation 4   General duty
Regulation 6   Work to an installation
Regulation 9   Prevention of fire and explosion
Regulation 13 General duty

Pipelines Safety (PSR) Regulations 1996[21]

Regulation 10 Work on pipeline

Pressure Systems Safety Regulations 2000[22]

Regulation 8   Written scheme of examination: measures necessary to prepare the pressure system for safe examination
Regulation 9   Examination in accordance with the written scheme

Provision and Use of Work Equipment Regulations 1998[23]

Regulation 19 Isolation from sources of energy
Regulation 22 Maintenance operations

Appendix 2 Further information on different permit types

1   It is important to realise that similar terminology may be used at different sites for types of permits which are fundamentally different. Some of the permits listed here may be called certificates. Clarity is essential to prevent confusion of permits-to-work with other kinds of document. It should be noted that in some permit-to-work systems, one permit may be designed to cover all of those described below.

Hot work permit

2   Hot work is usually taken to apply to an operation that could include the application of heat or ignition sources to tanks, vessels, pipelines etc which may contain or have contained flammable vapour, or in areas where flammable atmospheres may be present. Hot work permits, typically coloured red or red-edged, are more generally applied to any type of work which involves actual or potential sources of ignition and which is done in an area where there may be a risk of fire or explosion, or which involves the emission of toxic fumes from the application of heat. They are normally used for any welding or flame cutting, for the use of any tools which may produce sparks and for the use of any electrical equipment which is not intrinsically safe or of a suitably protected type. Some sites or installations distinguish between high energy sources of ignition like naked flames, welding and spark-producing grinding wheels, which are almost certain to ignite flammable atmospheres, and low energy sources like hand tools and non-sparking portable electrical equipment, which are likely to cause ignition only if there is a fault. In some cases, to differentiate between these tasks, fire and naked flame certificates or electrical certificates have been used, to minimise the risk of electric shock to people carrying out any work on electrical equipment.

Cold work permit

3   Cold work permits, typically blue-edged or coloured blue, are frequently used to cover a variety of potentially hazardous activities which are not of a type covered by a hot work permit. The activities for which a cold work permit may be appropriate will vary from site to site but should be clearly defined.

Electrical work permit

4   An electrical permit-to-work is primarily a statement that a circuit or item of equipment is safe to work on. A permit should not be issued on equipment that is live. Further guidance on electrical work permits is given in *Electricity at work: Safe working practices* HSG85.[24]

Equipment disjointing certificate/breaking containment permit

5   This type of certificate is used for any operation that involves disconnecting equipment or pipe work that contains (or has contained) any hazardous or high-pressure fluids or other substances. This type of certificate will normally be used for the insertion of spades into pipe work, and for the removal of such spades. These permits are typically black-edged.

Confined spaces entry certificate

6   Confined space entry certificates (unless detailed on a hot work or cold work permit) are used to specify the precautions to be taken to eliminate exposure to dangerous fumes or to an oxygen-depleted atmosphere before a person is permitted to enter a confined space. The certificate should confirm that the space is free from dangerous fumes or asphyxiating gases. It should also recognise the possibility of fumes desorbing from residues, oxygen depletion of the atmosphere as a result of oxidation, or the ingress of airborne contaminants from adjacent sources. The certificate should specify the precautions to be taken to protect the enclosed atmosphere against these hazards, eg by forced ventilation, physical isolation or by the provision of personal protective equipment including breathing apparatus.

Machinery certificate

7   This type of certificate is used for work on large, complex items of machinery to ensure correct isolation before the work is carried out.

Isolation certificate

8   This type of certificate may be very similar to a machinery certificate or an electrical certificate. It is usually used as a means of ensuring that the particular equipment is mechanically and electrically isolated before it is worked on. It is possible that a similarly named certificate may be used for chemical isolation of plant before work is done on it or entry is made. If so, these should be cross-referenced to associated permits.

Excavation certificate/heavy equipment movement certificate

9   This may also be called a 'ground disturbance permit' or something similar. It will typically be required whenever any digging, excavation or boring has to be done, to ensure that no underground services or pipe work will be affected eg by damage or subsidence. The movement or placing of heavy equipment may also cause damage.

Radiation certificate

10   Radiation certificates, typically coloured yellow, outline necessary control measures to minimise risks of exposure to radioactive sources including site inspection, controls on source exposure, access or containment barriers and radiation monitoring.

Diving certificate

11   Diving certificate can be used to control the diving activity itself and to ensure that there are no other activities taking place nearby which create unnecessary additional risks (eg over-side work, live firewater intake pumps).

Control of less hazardous work

12   The lowest level of control within a safe system of work involves 'routine duties', where assessed, detailed and approved work instruction or procedures define work that can be undertaken on site (eg process operators changing filters). Some offshore sites may use a 'T-card' or other simplified certificate to enable less hazardous work to be integrated with other more hazardous work (eg changing filters near hot work).

Appendix 3 Checklist for the assessment of permit-to-work systems

1   The purpose of this checklist is to help everyone concerned with the preparation of permit-to-work systems to decide whether a permit-to-work system covers all the points which are considered essential in this guidance. The checklist is intended for use when setting up a new permit-to-work system or when auditing an existing system.

Policy

2   Is there a clearly laid down policy for risk assessment of high-hazard operational and maintenance activities and their control procedures?

3   Are the objectives of the permit system clearly defined and understood?

4   Is the permit system flexible enough to allow it to be applied to other potentially hazardous work, apart from that which may have been specifically identified when the system was established?

Organising
Control
5   Are responsibilities for the following made clear:

- Management of the permit-to-work system?
- Permit form design and system scope?
- Type of jobs subject to permit?
- Control of contractors?

6   Are the types of work, or areas where permits must be used, clearly defined and understood by all concerned?

7   Is it clearly laid down who may issue permits?

8   Is it clearly laid down how permits should be obtained for specific jobs?

9   Are people prevented from issuing permits to themselves?

10   Is the permit system recognised throughout the site or installation as being essential for certain types of work?

11   Are copies of permits issued for the same equipment/area kept and displayed together?

12   Is there a means of co-ordinating all work activities to ensure potential interactions are identified?

13   Is there provision on the permit form to cross-reference other relevant certificates and permits?

14   Is there a means to ensure other people who could be affected by the proposed work give their agreement before the work (or preparations for it) is started?

15   Where there are isolations common to more than one permit, is there a procedure to prevent the isolation being removed before all the permits have been signed off?

16   If an electronic system is in place, is a valid means available to recover the co-ordination of work activities in the event of the electronic system failing?

Communication
17   Does the system provide both for the recipient to retain the permit and for a record of live permits and suspended permits to be maintained at the point of issue?

18   Does the system require a copy of the permit to be displayed at the workplace?

19   Do permits clearly specify the job to be done?

20   Do permits clearly specify whom they are issued to?

21   Do permits clearly specify the plant or geographical area to which work must be limited?

22   Does the recipient have to sign the permit to show that they have both read and understood the hazards and control measures detailed in the permit?

23   Do permits clearly specify a time limit for expiry or renewal?

24   Does the permit include a handover mechanism for work which extends beyond a shift or other work period, including work which has been suspended?

25   Is a hand-back signature required when the job is complete?

Training and competence

26   Is the permit system thoroughly covered during site or installation safety induction training?

27   Are personnel who have special responsibilities under

the permit system, eg issuing and isolating authorities, properly authorised and trained?

28 Do these people have sufficient time to carry out their duties properly?

29 Does the permit system require formal assessment of personnel competence before they are given responsibilities under the permit procedure?

30 Is a record of training and competence maintained?

31 Do training and competence requirements include contractors with responsibilities under the permit-to-work system?

32 Are individuals provided with written confirmation of completion of relevant training, and are these documents checked before appointments are made within the permit-to-work system?

33 Do authorised issuers have sufficient knowledge about the hazards associated with relevant plant?

Planning and implementation

34 Does the permit clearly specify the job to be undertaken?

35 Is there a set of properly documented isolation procedures for use when working on potentially hazardous items of plant, and do they provide for long-term isolation?

36 Is there a clear requirement for work being done under a permit to be stopped if site conditions change or any new hazards have arisen?

37 Does the permit contain clear rules about how the job should be controlled or abandoned in the event of an emergency?

38 Does the permit system require any potential hazards at the work site to be clearly identified and recorded on the permit?

39 Does the permit clearly specify the precautions to be taken by permit users and other responsible people?

40 Is there a procedure to identify and monitor tasks which require inhibiting safety devices, eg fire and gas detectors, to

ensure that contingency plans and precautions are in place?

Measuring performance

41 Is there a monitoring procedure or are there scheduled spot checks to ensure that permits are being followed?

Audit and review

42 Is there a procedure for reporting any incidents that have arisen during work carried out under a permit?

43 Is the permit-to-work system audited as appropriate, preferably by people not normally employed at the site or offshore installation?

44 Is there a procedure for reviewing the permit system at defined intervals?

Appendix 4 Permit-to-work monitoring checklist

1   This checklist is intended to be used for the day-to-day monitoring of permits in use.

Date:	Time:	Active:
Permit type:	Reference number:	Complete:
Reviewer:	Position:	Installation:
Appended certificates: (list)		

If any unsafe conditions are found, the work must be stopped and the issuing authority and the performing authority notified immediately.

	Yes	No	N/A
1 Is the scope of work clearly specified?			
2 Are necessary risk assessments available for review?			
3 Are identified hazards listed on the permit-to-work?			
4 Are appropriate precautions listed on the permit-to-work (including clearly specified isolations)?			
5 Is the operational time limit of the permit clear? (Are extensions properly authorised?)			
6 Are certificates completed properly and appended to the permit?			
7 Are other area or system activities cross-referenced correctly via the permit?			
8 Are copies of permits, certificates and attachments legible?			
9 Are signatures and initials traceable and legible?			
10 Are copies of permits and certificates posted at correct locations?			
11 Are attachments, drawings etc held at the correct locations?			
12 Are users briefed on the permit-to-work, and have they acknowledged understanding of requirements?			
13 Do people know what to do in the event of emergency?			
14 Are isolations appropriate for the task, clearly specified on the permit or isolation certificate, and correctly implemented?			
15 Are common isolations cross-referenced?			

	Yes	No	N/A
16 Are the right people aware of isolated equipment?			
17 Is the area authority aware of the work?			
18 Is the work carried out in conformance with the permit?			
19 Are control measures and personal protective equipment appropriate for the task?			
20 Are tools and equipment suitable and in good condition?			
21 Are housekeeping standards satisfactory?			

Comments:	
Reviewer:	Signature:
Performing authority:	Signature:

References and further reading

References

1 *The safe isolation of plant and equipment* Guidance HSE Books 1997 ISBN 0 7176 0871 9

2 *Task Risk Assessment Guide* Step Change In Safety (www.stepchangeinsafety.net)

3 *The public inquiry into the Piper Alpha disaster* Command paper Cm. 1310 The Stationery Office 1990 ISBN 0 10 113102 X

4 http://www.scotcourts.gov.uk/opinions/KING.html

5 *Management of Health and Safety at Work Regulations 1999* SI 1999/3242 The Stationery Office 1999 ISBN 0 11 085625 2

6 *Health and Safety at Work etc Act 1974 Ch37* The Stationery Office 1974 ISBN 0 10 543774 3

7 *Reducing error and influencing behaviour* HSG48 (Second edition) HSE Books 1999 ISBN 0 7176 2452 8

8 *Health and Safety at Work etc Act 1974 (Application outside Great Britain) Order 1995* SI 1995/263 The Stationery Office 1995 ISBN 0 11 052413 6

9 *Confined Spaces Regulations 1997* SI 1997/1713 The Stationery Office 1997 ISBN 0 11 064643 6

10 *Control of Major Accident Hazards Regulations 1999* SI 1999/743 The Stationery Office 1999 ISBN 0 11 082192 0

11 *Control of Substances Hazardous to Health Regulations 2002* SI 2002/2677 The Stationery Office 2002 ISBN 0 11 042919 2

12 *Dangerous Substances and Explosive Atmospheres Regulations 2002* SI 2002/2776 The Stationery Office 2002 ISBN 0 11 042957 5

13 *Electricity at Work Regulations 1989 SI 1989/635* The Stationery Office 1989 ISBN 0 11 096635 X

14 Memorandum of guidance on the Electricity at work Regulations 1989. Guidance on Regulations HSR25 HSE Books 1989 ISBN 0 7176 1602 9

15 *Ionising Radiations Regulations 1999* SI 1999/3232 The Stationery Office 1999 ISBN 0 11 085614 7

16 *Lifting Operations and Lifting Equipment Regulations 1998* SI 1998/2307 The Stationery Office 1998 ISBN 0 11 079598 9

17 *Offshore Installations (Prevention of Fire and Explosion, and Emergency Response) Regulations 1995* SI 1995/743 The Stationery Office 1995 ISBN 0 11 052751 8

18 *Offshore Installations (Safety Case) Regulations 1992* SI 1992/2885 The Stationery Office 1992 ISBN 0 11 025869 X

19 *Offshore Installations and Pipeline Works (Management and Administration) Regulations 1995* SI 1995/738 The Stationery Office 1995 ISBN 0 11 052735 6

20 *Offshore Installations and Wells (Design and Construction etc) Regulations 1996* SI 1996/913 The Stationery Office 1996 ISBN 0 11 054451 X

21 *Pipelines Safety Regulations 1996* SI 1996/825 The Stationery Office 1996 ISBN 0 11 054373 4

22 *Pressure Systems Safety Regulations 2000* SI 2000/128 The Stationery Office 2000 ISBN 0 11 085836 0

23 *Provision and Use of Work Equipment Regulations 1998* SI 1998/2306 The Stationery Office 1998 ISBN 0 11 079599 7

24 *Electricity at work: Safe working practices* HSG85 (Second edition) HSE Books 2003 ISBN 0 7176 2164 2

Further reading

Management of health and safety at work. Management of Health and Safety at Work Regulations 1999. Approved Code of Practice and guidance L21 (Second edition) HSE Books 2000 ISBN 0 7176 2488 9

Safe work in confined spaces. Confined Spaces Regulations 1997. Approved Code of Practice, Regulations and guidance L101 HSE Books 1997 ISBN 0 7176 1405 0 Printed and published by the Health and Safety Executive

Further information

HSE priced and free publications are available by mail order from HSE Books, PO Box 1999, Sudbury, Suffolk CO10 2WA Tel: 01787 881165 Fax: 01787 313995 Website: www.hsebooks.co.uk (HSE priced publications are also available from bookshops and free leaflets can be downloaded from HSE's website: www.hse.gov.uk.)

For information about health and safety ring HSE's Infoline Tel: 0845 345 0055 Fax: 02920 859260 e-mail: hseinformationservices@natbrit.com or write to HSE Information Services, Caerphilly Business Park, Caerphilly CF83 3GG.

The Stationery Office publications are available from The Stationery Office, PO Box 29, Norwich NR3 1GN Tel: 0870 600 5522 Fax: 0870 600 5533 e-mail: customer.services@tso.co.uk Website: www.tso.co.uk (They are also available from bookshops.)